Motorcycle Tours in the South of Ireland

Motorcycle Tours
in the
South of Ireland

BARTH BUCKLEY
PATRICK NORDSTROM

MERCIER PRESS

MERCIER PRESS
Douglas Village, Cork, Ireland
www.mercierpress.ie

Trade enquiries to Columba Mercier Distribution,
55a Spruce Avenue, Stillorgan Industrial Park, Blackrock, Dublin

ISBN 1 85635 493 8

10 9 8 7 6 5 4 3 2 1

Mercier Press receives financial assistance from
the Arts Council/An Chomhairle Ealaíon

Printed and Bound by ColourBooks Ltd

Contents

Thanks	9
Foreword	11
Recommended maps	13
Worth a trip	15
Safety first	17
A short note about driving on Irish roads	20
The 'right' bike for Irish roads	26
Some tips	28
Cork to Kenmare	33
Cork to Killorglin	35
Cork to Glenflesk	37
Cork to Castleisland	39
Cork to Castleisland, a variation	41
Cork to Bantry Bay	43
The Nagles Mountains	45
Cork to Kilmallock	47
The Vee	49
Cork to Clonmel	52
The River Run	54
Cork to Ballyvourney	57
Ballyvourney around the Paps	59
Ballyvourney and Macroom	61
Cork to Baltimore	63
Cork to Mizen Head	65
Cork to Sheep's Head	67

Cork to Sheep's Head, a variation   69

Cork to the Ring of Beara   73

Cork to Allihies   75

Cork to Waterville   80

Cork to Kenmare, a variation   82

Cork to Dingle   86

Tralee to Dingle   88

Macroom to the Paps   91

Ring of Kerry   94

Cork to Listowel   96

Cork to Foynes   99

Cork to Foynes, a variation   101

The 'big one' – a five-day trip   104

Where to sleep   115

What you should see   117

A note about ancient Ireland   129

'Butter on the road'   132

Always expect the unexpected   135

Travelling to Ireland   138

Very last words   141

To my family, Amy and Kim, and all my friends:
now you know where I have been all these years

– Barth Buckley

To my children, Henrik and Lisa,
... one day you will understand daddy's
excitement about motorcycling

To Ma, with thanks for your support

And to everyone who shares the joys of
biking and Ireland with me

– Patrick Nordstrom

Thanks

I would like to thank my friend and co-author, Barth Buckley. His knowledge of all the routes and ways made this book possible. For many years Barth has shown the beauty and wildness of this island to countless motorcycle-tourists. Of course that doesn't stop him from driving to the Alps at least once a year ...

Many thanks to all who made this book a reality, and in particular to: Mary Feehan and the team at Mercier Press, Dana Wilk, who established the contacts in Germany, and all the friends with whom we have enjoyed numerous spins.

– Patrick Nordstrom

Foreword

Fáilte, fans of Ireland, and those of you who soon will be. This book is about the 'secret' routes, as they are known by the locals, away from the main roads in addition to the 'typical' tours, such as the ring of Kerry, We, that is Barth and myself, concentrate on these routes in the south and south-west of Ireland. This part of Ireland is so full of spectacular routes that it would be impossible to see them all over one summer season.

We have concentrated on describing the most scenic and most interesting routes in biking terms, as well as routes of historic interest. The risk of finding boring routes, i.e. straight ones, is almost non-existent in Ireland.

The descriptions in this book are limited to the necessary directions. We are unable to mention all the towns and villages along the way as this would take up too much space, and it would also take away your sense of adventure and discovery. When you are on the road here you will realise that every stop you make will be a special one and if you want more information on a place all you have to do is ask a local, or enquire in the nearest information office – the pub. They will be more than happy to help.

All the routes are recommended and they can be varied according to individual needs and taste. It is helpful that the south of Ireland has more roads per square mile than anywhere in the world. If you feel the route you have chosen is not driveable for some reason, you can find an alternative route just around the next corner. For some bikes it is possible to avoid the more difficult routes and meet up again in the next village.

Don't expect a lot of splendid photographs in this book: although we always carry a camera with us and Barth has included some good pictures from previous trips around Ireland, we usually try not to stop along the way. The photographs are to give you a flavour of the scenery of Ireland ... Anyway, it is your job to take your own photos! Barth and I can tell you where the right spots are.

Since coming to Ireland for the first time in 1991, I've been commuting from Germany sometimes as many as six times a year. I was spending so much time here that I decided to move to Ireland in 2004. In my case the old Irish saying is true:

Traveller, when you come to Ireland,
be prepared to come back.
You will lose a piece of your heart here and you will
always return to find it.

Barth has had the privilege of always having been here ...

– Patrick and Barth
Ireland, January 2006

Recommended maps

All the routes described in this book can be found in the 1:50,000 maps of the Ordnance Survey of Ireland. They might be somewhat unwieldy to handle but in terms of precision and resolution they are second to none. Of course any other maps can be used, but most of the routes described are not to be found in a lesser resolution.

From the 1:50,000 series we recommend, dependent on routes, map numbers: 63, 64, 70, 71, 72, 73, 74, 78, 79, 80, 81, 83, 84, 85, 86, 87, 88 and 89.

We also recommend using a compass.

These maps can be found in most newspaper shops. Petrol stations usually provide maps for the local region. If you would like to plan your tour at home, Barth and I can help you to obtain the maps needed: at the end of the book you'll find our contact details.

Worth a trip

In a well-known motorcycle tour guide the driving conditions in the Alps are described as 'motorcycle heaven'. Most people will confirm that it is the opposite in Ireland.

Motorcyclists from other countries who are accustomed to smooth wide roads with a good grip to their surface come to Ireland and face challenges, which either bring tears to their eyes or a grin to their faces.

This is what motorcycling is all about; the excitement, the adventure, the challenge of navigating your way through these tracks, which are rather politely referred to as public roads.

In its favour there is also the overwhelming beauty of the landscape, the warmth of the people and its proximity to the rest of Europe.

When you come here you will know what we are talking about:

'we had a hell of a good time!'

Safety first

Here is some advice for motorcyclists who intend coming to Ireland. We don't want to seem 'wise guys' but safety is our main concern. Ireland demands more from bikers than we are used to in other parts of Europe.

We recommend that only the more experienced rider visit Ireland, not only because of the bad road conditions, but also because of the lack of awareness that many car drivers have of motorcyclists in traffic here. A major problem here is that car drivers don't use their mirrors enough.

First a short note on the road conditions (more on this in the next chapter). Even smaller roads in most parts of Europe are generally well maintained with a good road surface. If the surface is in exceptionally bad condition, there are usually warning signs. Not so in Ireland (yet).

Until the 1980s Ireland was a relatively poor country and it is only in recent years that motorcycles over 250cc have become popular. Most of the modern bikes are overpowered for the Irish roads. With a speed limit of 100 kph (120 kph on the motorway), and the poor road conditions, modern sports bikes are not driven to their full capacity.

I am sorry to say that in recent years accidents involving high-powered sports bikes have become more common. High output

engines, careless car drivers, bad road conditions and alcohol all contribute to the number of accidents.

We therefore recommend:

No alcohol

For some of the Irish road conditions full concentration and maximum reaction are a must for a safe journey. The Guinness tastes better after the journey, not before.

No speeding

You have to adapt your speed to suit the road conditions. If you drive too fast, besides the danger, you will miss the beautiful

landscape. By the way, you will soon find out that the 80/100 kph speed limits are not necessary as the road itself imposes its own limits ... Driving in Ireland, apart from driving on the left, demands a special discipline and skill.

Drive on the left!

In Ireland you drive on the left hand side of the road. For those who are not used to this, it is a good idea to put a highly visible sign on your bike to remind you to drive on the left. It is very easy to forget this, especially in the morning, after a break, after lunch and after getting petrol. By the way, when driving on the left you must yield to the traffic coming from the right.

A short note about driving on Irish roads

All roads described in this book are public roads. What is charming for some about Irish roads can be a nightmare for others. Some secondary roads can be in poor condition. The so-called potholes can be deep enough to damage wheel rims and cause the rider to lose control of the bike. On rarely used roads you can find fallen trees blocking your way. Some roads have severe bumps and dips. Often the reason for this is that the roads were once just old tracks which were tarmacked over without proper foundations. Rainwater washes away the ground causing the road to sink in places and leaving some of these roads like roller coasters.

By the way, there are no individual warning signs for these road conditions – in this country people must be aware that potholes and bumps are everywhere. And so many signs do not exist ...

As the roads usually follow the natural contours of the landscape, there are a lot of dips and on a seemingly straight empty road you can meet another vehicle coming up out of one of these dips. Another danger is when the visible part of the road seems to bend to the left, and as you approach the bend you realise that the road takes a turn to the right first but this is obscured by a dip in the road (or vice versa). Such a dip recently cost an over-enthusiastic biker his bike and nearly his life.

In the south in particular the stone walls at the edge of the road are covered with green vegetation, which gives the landscape a romantic touch. However, this is a big disadvantage when trying to orientate a bike. Moreover, it makes it impossible to look into the bends, especially left hand corners. You have to be prepared for surprises in and after every bend: loose chippings, potholes, dirt, farm machinery, cows and sheep just to name a few.

The smaller the road the slower the speed

Distance and arrival time cannot be calculated with continental measurements. For Irish travel time you must add at least fifty per cent more journey time (100 km = 1½ hours).

The narrower the road gets, the wider the oncoming vehicles get – especially the trucks in bends!

Before a bend which you cannot see into
– and most of them are like this –
slow down and keep to the left

... and don't insist on being right when the oncoming vehicle is bigger than you. It is better to argue afterwards than not at all.

In the wet, and this is the case a lot of the time, the grass strip in the centre of the tracks can be very slippery. You should choose a speed at which you can stay between the grass centre and the edge of the road. If you have to cross this grassy patch, you should reduce your speed and keep the bike as upright as possible.

Beware of the grass strip!

Driving in Ireland takes one hundred per cent concentration. It is very difficult to watch the road and watch the scenery at the same time: if you are not careful, you will be in the scenery. Frequent stops are in order. The landscape is well worth a look.

If the landscape is worth looking at, **stop** and **look**
So leave enough time for frequent stops in your journey

Try not to depend too much on the road signs in rural areas. Some signs get turned the wrong way by the wind, being hit by trucks and by the local youth. It is advisable to carry a map with you, and be able to read it, and a compass – especially for those days when the sun is hiding behind the clouds. A GPS would be a blessing, but don't worry, you can ask any of the locals and they will be happy to help. Remember:

Ireland is a small country – you might not
know where you are but you never get lost

Be especially cautious approaching villages on Sundays: people here enjoy a local game called ROAD BOWLING. The villagers

enjoy playing (and betting on) this sport. So it is not unusual to meet a large crowd on the road.

You are even more likely to meet one of the many vintage rallies during the summer season: owners of vintage cars and bikes are proud of their vehicles and love to gather to share their enthusiasm in their hobby. But when you meet a rally of this kind, especially when it is of old bikes, bear in mind the following:

Most old motorcycles do not have any mirrors or indicators and the brakes are quite poor compared to modern standards. You should therefore leave plenty of room and be extra cautious if you intend to overtake.

However you will find they are very welcoming if you wish to meet up with the rally at one of the various stopping points.

As we have said already, driving in Ireland requires even more concentration than in most other countries. But if you can cope with these conditions you will be repaid with beautiful surroundings, scenic landscape, warm and friendly people and a vibrant mix of old and new culture.

The 'right' bike for Irish roads

Those who are in control of their bike should manage almost all situations. However, many of the roads described here are basically nothing more than tracks with a grassy strip in the middle, which snake their way over the landscape.

Enduro/Trail Bikes, which have high torque, wide handlebars, are lightweight and have narrow tyres are the ideal bikes for these conditions ... that doesn't mean to say that you can't ride on these roads with other bikes ... A Pan European & Yamaha Diversion have managed to travel all these routes.

To make life easier for you we have categorised the routes as follows:

easy   =   all bikes

medium   =   difficult for sports bikes and heavy
                         touring bikes (challenging)

difficult   =   not recommended for sports bikes or
                         heavy touring bikes

There are plenty of roads to suit all bikes.
but sometimes there is no road at all ...

Some tips

When is the best time to travel?

We would suggest all year. While the bikers on the continent have to store away their bikes for the winter, we have virtually snow free winters in Ireland. There is a reason why palm trees grow here. Yes, palm trees! The reason is the gulf stream which creates a very mild climate and makes a perfect environment for palm trees to grow in, especially in the south.

The tourist season starts at the beginning of April and finishes at the end of September. In March and October, though, the weather can be very pleasant, the landscape changes into its winter colours, or still has them, the roads are much quieter and accommodation is much cheaper. Here in the south we ride our bikes all year.

Petrol stations and repairs

95 octane is the standard petrol sold here. Filling stations are plentiful and you will be pleased to note that petrol is still much cheaper here than in the rest of the continent.

Most of the major towns have a motorcycle repair shop. If you need to find a motorcycle shop, just ask another biker or any of the locals should be able to point you in the right direction. Don't be afraid of the 'Irish repairs' – although often improvised, they get the job done!

Calling home

Ireland was one of the first countries in Europe to have a full digital network coverage (years before Germany). Your mobile (or cell phone) will find coverage in most areas.

Staying overnight

B&Bs (Bed and Breakfast) come well recommended (only with rare exceptions). The advantage of B&Bs is that they are privately run and it is not unusual to meet the family. They are usually delighted to help with suggestions and hints for your continuing travel arrangements, as well as local knowledge and stories. Prices are governed by the time of year and location. Naturally, prices are going to be higher in typical tourist regions like Killarney than 20 km outside of the town.

There are also around 100 campsites in Ireland and this number is growing all the time. If you prefer to camp in the countryside, be sure to ask the landowner for permission.

Money

Coming from one of the European community member states there is no need for changing money because Ireland is also a member state, and the euro is the national currency.

At every bank link you can draw money with an EC-card.

Immigration

If you are from an EU state and travelling to Ireland, you won't usually encounter any problems. If you're coming from France and wanting to pass through England you will find that the border controls are more thorough. And, if your love for Ireland gets you stuck here, you should be aware that vehicles which are being used for more than 6 months in this country have to be registered and taxed here. It is tax free to import your own vehicle if you have owned it for more than a year. Your local revenue commissioner can tell you about any other charges.

Road signs and speed limits

For some years the metric system has been the official standard in Ireland, which means that the distances shown on the road signs are in kilometres, unless they are the 'old' signs, identifiable as white with a black rim and prominent black letters: here the distance is still shown in miles (conversion about 1:1.6 – so 10 miles are about 16 km). All of these signs should have been changed to kilometres in 2005. If you ask an Irishman he will usually answer you with 'imperial' measures, that is miles, yards, feet, inches, gallons, etc. Old habits die hard ...

In 2005, speed signs were changed to kilometres:

	Old	New
through villages	30 mph	(48 kph) 50 kph
occasionally	40 mph	(64 kph)
secondary roads	50 mph	80 kph
main roads	60 mph	(96 kph) 100 kph
motorways	70 mph	(112 kph) 120 kph

Speeding is controlled vigorously, minimum fine is € 50.

As I have said most of the roads driven by us impose their own limits, which you will appreciate when you are driving them.

Route recommendations

The numbers refer to the map number of the Ordnance Survey, Discovery Series, 1:50,000. Most routes are round trips – that shouldn't prevent anyone from combining one route with another, or just using them as a rough guide.

Some of the routes are described by Barth in his own inimitable style, so I hope you enjoy him taking you along for the ride for some of our most enjoyable trips!

Enough chat, let's get on the road!

Cork to Kenmare

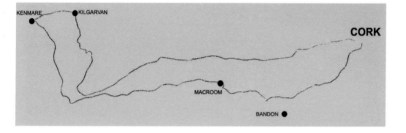

The starting point is the N22, in the direction of Macroom and Killarney, at Cork County Hall. This building is Cork's highest and ugliest. Its location on the River Lee however, is beautiful.

Local motorcyclists meet at the petrol station not far from the County Hall on Sundays for a cup of coffee, a chat and a bit of a spin. Historically farmers in West Cork brought their goods, in particular butter, by horse and carriage to the market in Cork, hence the South Butter Road. Despite appearing straight on the map, the road follows the landscape through valleys and over passes and as a result there are sudden steep drops and climbs. Take the N22 west, turn left at Ovens Bridge, drive over Kilcrea Bridge (which crosses the River Bride) to Aherla. Proceed to Crookstown, through Kilmurry, Teerelton and Kilmichael to Inchigeelagh. Before coming to Inchigeelagh, go left through

Curraheen, passing a Mass Rock, and on to Toorenalour, Gort-loughra, through the Sheehy Mountains to Kealkill.

From Kealkill go north, driving through Conigar and over the Knockmanagh Hill towards Killgarvan, where you will cross the Priest's Leap. There is an interesting story behind the Priest's Leap: at a time when the Irish weren't allowed, amongst other things, to practise their religion, the priests and their community would meet in spots where they could overlook the landscape and identify approaching strangers in time to escape in the opposite direction. The iron cross marks such a place.

On the R569 turn left to Kenmare. To return to Cork take the R569 to Clonkeen and get on to the N22 here to Macroom and Cork.

Cork to Killorglin

Passes and scenic landscape
Category: medium
78/79/85/86

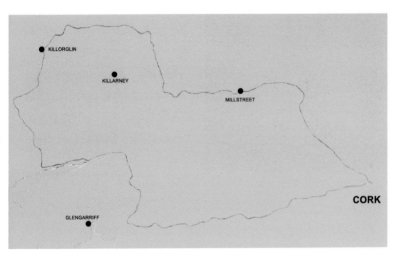

Killorglin is known for its numerous fairs and the journey there is spectacular. From the Cork County Hall take the road to Carrigrohane, Aherla, Stickstown to Crookstown. Here you take the R585 which brings you to Bealnablath, the place where Irish freedom fighter and statesperson Michael Collins was shot. The monument here is a reminder of the darker side of Irish history.

Proceed on the R585 through Cappeen and Shanlaragh, along the Cousane Gap. This is a very nice road to wag the bike through the bends, preferably in dry conditions though. In the village of Kealkill turn to the right, then take the next left: this road brings you northwards through Gougane Barra Forest Park, passing the spectacular Knocknamanagh Hill, and heading on towards Kilgarvan.

In Kilgarvan turn left on the R569, through Kenmare on the N70, and then through Templenoe until the sharp bend at the Lackeen Point. Here you turn right onto the small road which brings you over the Derreendarragh to the Ballaghbeama Gap in the Macgillycuddy's Reeks. Grand view! Continue through Boheeshil, take the next right, passing Lough Acoose to Killorglin. The way back to Cork goes over the N70 passing Milltown until shortly before Castlemaine, where you turn right onto the R561, continuing through Farranfore towards Scartaglin. Before the River Maine turn right following the river to Barraduff. Drive south for approximately 0.5 km on the R570 and take the next left to Caherbarnagh, passing Caherbarnagh Mountain, to Millstreet. From Millstreet drive eastwards to Lyre, where you turn south-east to Nad. From here the R579 brings you back to Cork quickly.

Cork to Glenflesk

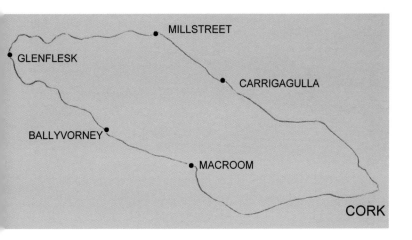

Though medium category, this is a relatively short spin which is nice for getting used to the different road conditions. Start at the Cork County Hall. Drive in the direction of the city, at the major crossroad turn left and left again on the R579 to Cloghroe. Turn right to Tower, through Matehy and Crean's Crossroads to Rylane Cross. Stay on the Kerry Road over Carrigagulla to Millstreet. This road is completely straight and rises and falls with the landscape. Long ago cart drivers could allow their horses to walk on straight whilst they slept along this road. The cart drivers used to make a stop at the Kerryman's Table before they went on with their load to the market in Cork. In Millstreet turn left at the church, this

road brings you to the west, alongside the Paps Mountains to Headfort. Turn left on the R570 to Glenflesk. From here take the N22 which brings you swiftly back to Cork.

Cork to Castleisland

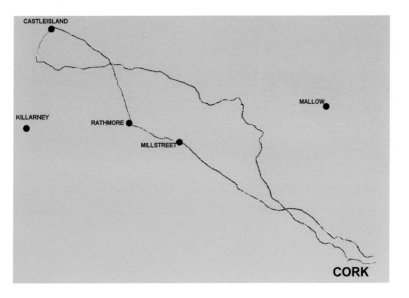

Start once again at the Cork County Hall. Drive in the direction of the city, at the major crossroad turn left and left again on the R579 to Cloghroe. Turn right to Tower, through Matehy and Crean's Crossroads to Rylane Cross. Stay on the Kerry Road through Carrigagulla to Millstreet. In Millstreet carry straight on joining the R582 to Rathmore. Before you get to the town centre in Rathmore turn right onto the very straight road to Coreencahill, Knockabout Cross, Cordal and Castleisland.

The way back brings you south to Currow, where you turn eastwards, passing Scartaglin, onto the R577 through Ballydesmond and Kishkeam to Cloonbannin and from here carry on to Banteer. In Banteer stay on the R579 back to Cork.

Cork to Castleisland Variation

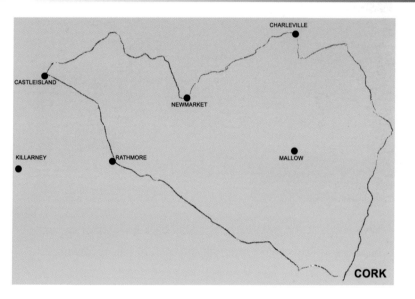

The starting point is the same as on the previous tours: the
Cork County Hall. Drive in the direction of the city, at the major
crossroad turn left and left again onto the R579 to Cloghroe.
Turn right to Tower, through Matehy and Crean's Crossroads to
Rylane Cross. Take the Kerry Road over Carrigagulla to Millstreet.
In Millstreet take the R582 to Rathmore. In Rathmore, before
you get to the town centre, turn right onto the very straight road
to Coreencahill, Knockabout Cross, Cordal and Castleisland. In
Castleisland cross the main road and you arrive at the Crag (Caves)
after a few miles. It's worthwhile stopping to see the caves and

have lunch at the restaurant. The way back brings you through Brosna and Rockchapel, after which you turn left in Newmarket to Charleville. The Kennedy Pub is worth a stop, especially in the evening when the nightclub opens. The last section is back through Ardpatrick, Kildorrey and Ballyhooly through the Nagles Mountains to Cork.

Cork to Bantry Bay

Passes and scenic landscapes
Category: medium, on dry days
85/86/89

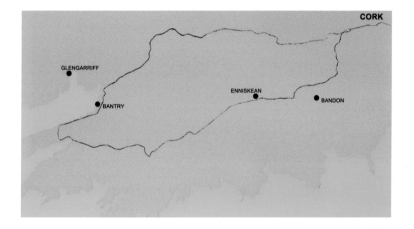

Start at Cork County Hall, follow the N22 in the direction of Macroom, turn left at the Ovens Bridge, in the direction of Cross Barry. Take the R589 to Kilpatrick, through Gash's and Tinkers crossroads to Carhoon, then cross the R586 to Gurteen. Proceed through Farrannasheshery, past Ballynacarriga, on the R637 and past the Curraghalicky Lake. In Drinagh turn right to Driminidy and Derreeny Bridge (Robin's Cross) on the R593. Take the R594 in the direction of Caheragh, but before the village you turn left to Glanaphuca through Barnaghgeehy and Durrus to Glanlough. Proceed to Clashadoo where you cross over the Sheep's Head Way to Rooska. Here you will find a beautiful view on Bantry Bay (see picture).

On the coast road turn to the right towards Bantry.

You will find many places to stay for the night around Bantry Bay. If you want to turn back to Cork, you might like to take the R584 – a nice road with a lot of bends to 'wiggle' your 'end'. Perfect for scratching the footrests. After the Pass of Keimaneigh (nice waterfall on the left hand side) we recommend a short excursion to the Gougane Barra Lake and Forest Park, the source of the River Lee.

Instead of driving on to Macroom and then onto the N22 to Cork (the easiest way) we recommend a nicer way, a parallel route to the south of the N22 through Carrignaneelagh, Kilmurry, Crookstown, Aherla and Cork.

The Nagles Mountains

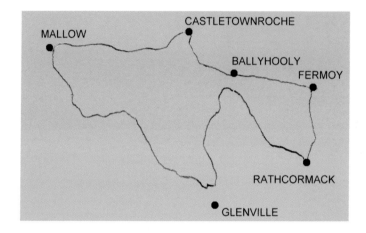

This tour is suitable as an easy warming up or between lunch and afternoon tea.

The start is in Fermoy, on the N8 to Rathcormack. In Rathcormack turn right to Ballyhooly. Near Cappagh you will find a very scenic view over the Blackwater Valley. At the roundabout before Ballyhooly take the second exit to Glenville, up the hill again. After about 12 km take first road to the right (before Glenville). At the Monee Crossroads take a right and after the left hand bend follow the road up the hill. At the top of the hill you will find a fantastic view over Mallow. At the t-junction turn left to

Mallow (if you turn right, you'll get to Killavullen). The way back to Fermoy is on the N72 through Castletownroche.

Cork to Kilmallock

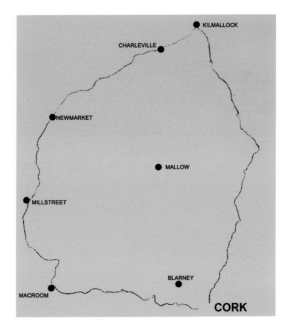

From the County Hall in Cork travel towards the city, at the first crossroads turn left and left again onto the R618 through Coachford to Macroom. At the village border turn right and right again, take the second right in the direction of Ballynagree. Before Ballynagree turn left to Carriganimmy. From here take the R582 to Millstreet. In Millstreet turn right onto the R583, after about 4 km turn left to Newmarket. In Newmarket turn onto

the R578 and then the R515 to Charleville and on to Kilmallock. In Kilmallock you will find the castle and the Old Mill with its working waterwheel both worth investigating.

The way back is on the R512 to Glanworth and from there to Ballyhooly. Here you drive south through the Nagles Mountains to Glenville and on the R614 to Cork.

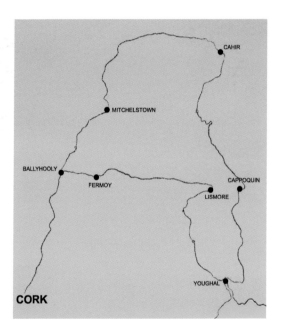

The start of this tour is the village of Ballyvolane in the north of Cork city. On the North Ring turn onto the New Road through White's Cross and onto the R614, then passing through Glenville, through the Nagles Mountains to Ballyhooly. From here carry on to Glanworth, and then turn right to Ballindangan and Mitchelstown. Carry on for a couple of kilometres on the R513 to

the north of Mitchelstown, then turn right towards Anglesborough and Barnai, around the Galty Mountains to Cahir.

The R668 from Cahir to Lismore is one of the best roads for bikers in the south of Ireland. The climb through a few well-designed bends ends in a breathtaking view, which opens up after the sharp bend. In good weather a stop is a must. The vista sweeps over several counties: County Tipperary straight ahead, County Limerick to the left of it and County Cork to the immediate left. Many years ago a certain Mr Grubb was buried standing upright not far from this spot: he wanted to have this view after his death forever more ... The Grubb monument is about 200m up the road from the bend on the left hand side. Top of the tour is the Sugartop Hill in the Knockmealdown Mountains, the shape of which gave the spot its name: the Vee. On dry weekends numerous motorcyclists enjoy taking the bends, watched by appreciative spectators.

After the Vee, turn left at the next crossroads onto the R669 to Cappoquin. Before Cappoquin turn left at the crossroads, towards the river. Here, not far from Cappoquin is the so-called Hindu Bridge: the bridge was built by the English in the nineteenth century in Indian style.

From Cappoquin follow the Blackwater River south to Youghal. The town itself is worth a stop but if it is baking hot the wide beach at Youghal will perhaps be even more attractive.

The way back is on the R634 to Tallow and Tallowbridge. After a short drive on the N72 you arrive at the charming medieval town of Lismore and the wonderful Lismore Castle is also worth visiting. If you like you can do the Vee a second time on the R668. Otherwise, the last section of the drive is on the R666, a very good road, to Fermoy and from here on the N8 brings you comfortably back to Cork.

Cork to Clonmel

Scenic route
Category: easy
80/81

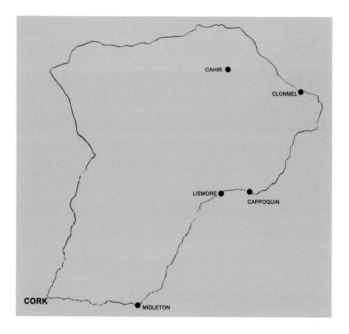

The start of this tour is again in Ballyvolane in the north of Cork City. On the North Ring turn right onto the New Road and drive through White's Cross on the R614, passing through Glenville, through the Nagles Mountains to Ballyhooly and Glanworth. In Glanworth turn left onto the R512 to Ardpatrick.

In Ardpatrick turn right to Kilfinnane and proceed in the direction of Galbally. On the R663 pass the Glen of Aherlow to Bansha.

Continue through Lagganstown and Newinn, and take the R687 there to Clonmel. The road through the Nier Valley alongside the Comeragh Mountains is spectacular. Further on to the west you'll get to Ballymacarbry. Here turn south onto the R671 to Ballynamult. Turn right to Ballynaguilkee and carry on to Cappoquin. Before Cappoquin you'll cross the river on the 'Hindu Bridge' (see previous tour). Travel alongside the Blackwater River to Lismore, where you will find the castle worth a visit. Continue through Tallowbridge and Tallow, and drive on to Midleton. From here you take the N25 back to Cork.

The River Run

Scenic landscapes
Category: easy
79/80/81

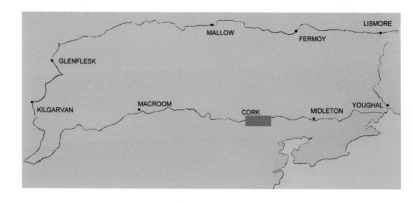

Start at the County Hall in Cork. Drive on the N22 out of the city, turn right at the next crossroads onto the R618 which follows the beautiful River Lee through Dripsey and Coachford to Macroom. Before the town of Macroom you cross the N22 and follow the very scenic R584 over Inchigeelagh and Ballingeary to Gougane Barra, about 5 km after Ballingeary, which is well signposted on the right.

As Gougane Barra is a dead end road, to proceed you go back to the R584 and turn right, over the Keimaneigh Pass to Kealkill. Here you take a sharp right, and then after about 100 m you come to a t-junction where you turn right again, over the Carriganass Bridge. At the ruined castle take a sharp left, this road climbs alongside the Comhola River up to Knocknamanagh. After the

Borlin Valley you can see Lough Akinkeen on the left hand side, an unusual bowl shaped lake between the hills. Go down on the other side of the mountain, turn right onto R569 just outside Kilgarvan you might visit the motor museum.

Proceed on the R569 to Clonkeen, turn left onto the N22 where you cross the Clodagh River on the Loo Bridge. This is an exciting road with a good surface which brings you through sweeping bends and fast straights to Glenflesk. At the church turn right onto the R570 to Barraduff where you turn right onto the N72, a fairly fast road, to Rathmore. After the village of Rathmore take the right hand turn, this is the R582 which takes you to Millstreet. Follow the R583 for about 3 km, turn right at Cooles Crossroad to Rathcool, Banteer and Lombardstown and then turn right onto the N72 which brings you to Mallow. Go straight through the roundabout and straight through the usually very lively town. At the clock house go straight ahead and after the bridge turn left, this very straight road is in good condition and takes you to Killavullen. In Killavullen take the second right, there is a sweeping bend to the east and then this road brings you to Ballyhooly. Some sections of the road follow the remains of an old railroad track. At the roundabout go left where you cross the Blackwater River again. From here you also have a good view on the Ballyhooly Castle on your left. After the bridge turn right and right again onto the N72. On the way to Fermoy you pass Hyde Castle and some of the more prominent stud farms in the country. Coming into Fermoy, turn right and take the first left before the bridge. Here the scenic R666 brings you through fantastic bends through Ballyduff to Lismore. From Lismore take the N72, which is an extremely good motorcycle road and follows the Blackwater to Cappoquin, where the river makes a dramatic turn to the south-east. Just outside Cappoquin turn right and follow the signposted road to Youghal. On the way there you pass the Strandcally Castle on your right. In Youghal where the Blackwater flows into the sea you might want to take a break, otherwise the N25 brings you through Midleton swiftly back to Cork.

Cork to Ballyvourney

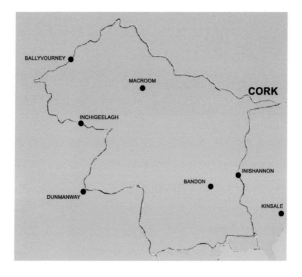

Start at the County Hall in Cork, take the N22 to the west, turn left at the Ovens Bridge, through Cross Barry to Inishannon. Proceed to the south through Ballinadee to Ballinspittle. Here you can take a diversion out to the Old Head of Kinsale. This piece of land ends in a privately owned Golf Club which isn't accessible to the public, but the view just before the entrance is worth the excursion, as are the beautiful beaches. From Ballinspittle proceed to the west on the R600 to Clonakilty.

Turn right onto the R588, through Knockskagh and Knocks to Enniskean. Turn left at Enniskean, then left onto the R586 to

Dunmanway. Before driving into the town turn right onto the R587 to Kilmichael, where the 'Kilmichael Ambush' took place. In the village turn left to Inchigeelagh.

If a good story interests you, you cannot pass Creedon's Hotel: the landlord there is a well-known 'storyteller' – and singer. If you manage to escape Creedon's Pub without getting drunk, you will probably want to continue your tour. Travel alongside Lough Allua to Ballingeary, turn right here to the north. Before the Inchee Bridge turn right towards the north-east, to Coolea and Ballyvourney. The road proceeds alongside the Derrynasaggart Mountains towards the north-east, crossing the R582 halfway between Millstreet and Carriganimmy. On the other side of the Derrynasaggart Mountains the road starts to climb again onto Musheramore. Turn right in the direction of Ballynagree (which the road passes in the south-west) alongside the Burren and then follow the road south-east to Peake. From here continue to Dripsey, then take the R618 to Cork.

Ballyvourney around the Paps

Scenic landscapes and more
Category: easy, some navigational challenge
79

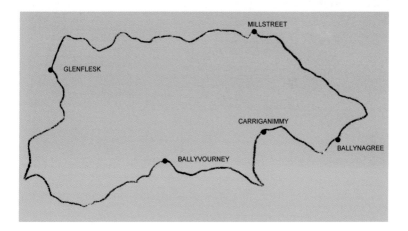

From Ballyvourney take a short run (approximately 1 km) on the N22 to Ballymakeery, then take the second left in the direction of Garrane. After about 5 km you turn left to Kilgobnet and Bawnatanaknock. After the Curraleigh Bridge turn right, and at the next t-junction turn left and then right onto the R582 to Carriganimmy. In Carriganimmy take the second left, up a small road. After Capeen Cross take the second left through Kilpatrick. After about 1.5 km the road turns sharply to the north-east and then brings you to Ballinagree. Continue to Carrigagulla Bridge where you turn left, and then left again at the t-junction in the direction of Millstreet. The road climbs up Musheramore and passes the Kerryman's Table. In Millstreet turn left at the church

and follow the road all the way alongside the Paps, through Caherbarnagh to Headfort. Turn left onto the R570 to Glenflesk, then turn left onto the N22. After about 2 km before Garries Bridge, turn right onto the R569. At Morley's Bridge turn left and follow the Roughty River up the mountain. On this road in Coom you pass Ireland's highest pub. Follow the road, passing Coolea and you get back to Ballyvourney.

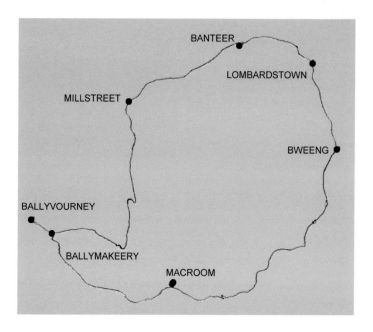

We start again in Ballyvourney and take the N22 into Ballymakeen, then turn right. After about 2 km turn left, left again, stay right at the farmhouse. At the next t-junction turn right and then next left into Kilnamartery. Turn left at Kilnamartery and first right at the side of the church, this will bring you all the way to Macroom. Turn left at the castle in Macroom, over the bridge and take the first right onto the R618. At the next junction at the mill stay right, then at the following junction stay left, through Carrigadrohid,

then take the next left and stay right at the following junction, until you come to Aghabullogue. After the church turn right onto R619, then go straight through at Crean's Crossroads, after which you will come to Donoughmore, Bweeng and further on to Lombardstown. In Lombardstown turn left to Banteer. In Banteer turn left again on the R579 to Nad. In Nad make a sharp turn to the right to Millstreet. In Millstreet turn left and left again, which is signposted to Macroom. After about 1 km on this road you will come to a grotto, stay left here when the road splits. When this road meets the R582 take a sharp right over the bridge, then next left and stay left again at next junction. Follow this road all the way down to Clondrohid, where you make a sharp turn to the right and follow this road back to Ballymakeery. Finally turn onto the N22 back to Ballavourney.

Cork to Baltimore

Scenic landscapes and more
Category: easy
86/87/88/89

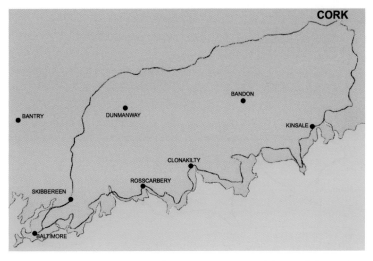

This tour brings you along the very scenic and beautiful south coast of County Cork. This time start at Johnstown, in the south of Cork.

Take the N28 onto the R611 to Carrigaline, Ballyfeard to Belgooly. Turn left onto the R600, through Kinsale, proceed on the R600 over the bridge and turn left onto the R604. As I've mentioned before the Old Head of Kinsale is a place of breathtaking beauty and worth an excursion here, despite the fact that the land's end is a private golf club and there is no public admission. Back up the hill again, opposite the crossroad, there is a monument to the sinking of the *Lusitania* in 1915 just off the Old Head of Kinsale.

In Ballinspittle go back onto the R600 to Timoleague and turn left here onto the R604 to Butlerstown, Ardgellane, North Ring and Clonakilty. As you leave Clonakilty turn south to Ardfield. On the land's end you will find the Galley Head lighthouse. Back on the road and your next stop is Castlefreke. A stop here is worthwhile, not only because of the Long Strand Beach with its dunes, but also for Rathbarry Castle and Castle Freke on the opposite side of the road. Drive on to Rosscarbery and continue through Cregg and Glandore to Union Hall, Rinneen, Castletownshend and Bawnlahan, after which you'll come to Baltimore. Here the castle of Baltimore is worth a visit and, if the weather is clear, you can also see Fastnet Rock in the south-west outside the coast, which is used as the turning point of the famous Fastnet Race. Using Baltimore as *your* turning point, take the R595 to Skibbereen, where you turn onto the R593 to Drimoleague and then take the R586 to Dunmanway. From here you turn onto the R585 to Crookstown, where you go right to Stickstown, Aherla and Cork.

Cork to Mizen Head

Scenic landscapes and scenic views
Category: easy
84/85/86/88/89

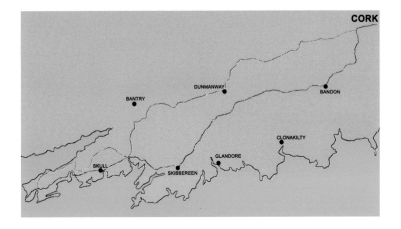

Begin the tour again at the Cork County Hall. Take the N22 west, turn left at Ovens Bridge and continue through Cross Barry on the R589 to Bandon. In Bandon take the R586 and as you drive out of the town take the first road to the left, through Kilcolman and Ballynacarriga, Curraghalicky and Carrigeeny Crossroads to Skibbereen. From Skibbereen you take the N71 to Ballydehob. Here take the westerly road to Ratheenroe, it will pass Mount Gabriel and go through Dunmanus, following the northern coastal line of the peninsula. From Dunmanus you follow the coast to Mizen Head. In clear weather you can see the Fastnet Rock in the south-east, which, as I mentioned before, is used as turning point during the Fastnet Regatta.

On the way back you take the R591 through Goleen. At Toormore turn right onto the R592 over Skull to Ballydehob. Turn left here on the N71 to Bantry. Before you come to Ardrah, turn right to Trawlebane, Glandart and Deelish and continue on to Dunmanway. Here take the R587 to Shanlaragh, turn right onto the R585 to Crookstown, and then turn right here to Stickstown, Aherla and Cork.

Cork to Sheep's Head

Beautiful landscape and two bays

Category: easy

79/80/86/87/88

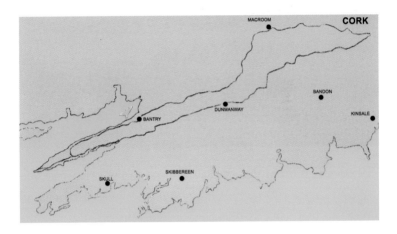

Start at the County Hall in Cork, again. Drive for around 2.5 km on the N22 out of the city, turn right at the next crossroads onto the R618 which follows the River Lee to Macroom. Before the town of Macroom turn left onto the N22, then take the next left again onto the R587. Follow this road until you have driven through the village of Shanlaragh. At the Ardcahan Bridge turn right and follow the road through the Mallabrackha Forest. Proceed in the direction of Farnanes, passing through Nowen Hill and follow the river Mealgh to Bantry. Here you take the coastal road over Relane Point, League Point and Collack to Kilcrohane. Turn right to the Sheep's Head. On the way back to Kilcrohane take the southerly coastal road, straight through Ahakista to Durrus. Cross over the

R591 and proceed through Ballycomane to the east where you cross over the N71 to the south of Ardrah. Further eastwards you will join the R586 to Dunmanway. After Dunmanway take the third to the left to Castletown. In Castletown you drive straight to the north where you get onto the R585. Turn right to Crookstown here, and right again through Stickstown and Aherla to Cork.

Cork to Sheep's Head Variation

Scenic landscape, mountains and a seagull
Category: medium
85/86/88

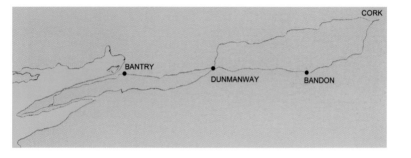

The weather was dry and overcast on this Sunday morning in May. The route that I had planned for today was from Cork to the Sheep's Head out on the Dunmanus peninsula and the arrangements were as usual, to meet in the filling station by the County Hall at 11 o'clock. Patrick arrived at my house at 9:30 for coffee and a chat. When I opened the garage door to get my bike out I discovered that Patrick's Pan had a flat tyre. On closer inspection having inflated the tyre, we discovered that it was punctured. At this stage I phoned Liam to tell him that we were running late. Thirty minutes later we had the puncture fixed and were on our way to the County Hall where Liam was waiting patiently for us.

We leave the filling station at 11:30 a.m. and head west on the N22, bypassing Ballincollig and driving on to Ovens where we

take a left turn at the Bridge Bar. From here we travel down to Killumney village and turn right. This road takes through Aherla, Cloughdubh and on to Crookstown, where we turned left onto the R585, the Bantry road. This road has quite a lot of bends for the first few miles, but if you get your speed right you can have great fun scratching through these corners. After these few miles of corners the road opens up to some very fast straight sections. This is an excellent motorcycling road with plenty of excitement for everyone. We travel through Coppeen and on in the direction of Bantry.

Next we turn left at Togher Bridge onto the Dunmanway road and after 2km we turn right at Keenragh Bridge up a small road. This road is quite narrow, so if you meet an oncoming car someone has to give way. There are some outstanding views of the surrounding mountains from here. At the next t-junction we turn right on the Dunmanway to Bantry road. Again this is a good fast road. At Castledonovan Bridge we turn right up a lovely mountain pass. At the top we stop for a break and take advantage of the breathtaking view. On a clear day you can see all the way down to Bantry Bay and Whiddy Island. From here we make our way quickly down past Lough Bofinna to Bantry. We stop for lunch in Vickery's Hotel where the staff are friendly and the food is good.

After a leisurely lunch we travel out on the N71 past the West Lodge Hotel and take a right turn to the Sheep's Head Peninsula. This is a beautiful part of West Cork where we climb from sea level all the way to Goat's Path, which is the highest point on the peninsula. Here you can look out over Bantry Bay on the one side and Dunmanus Bay on the other. If you ever travel down here you will understand why it's called the Goat's Path. Near the top we turn right on to a small road which is no more than a bumpy dirt track, but well worth the effort. Eventually we come to a t-junction on the south side of the peninsula. Here we turn right and travel the winding road out to Sheep's Head. We park in the car park at the end of this road, get a coffee from the café and sit in the sun looking out to sea.

While sitting here we notice a tame seagull wandering around the car park looking for food. Later we found out that the seagull's name is Joey and is a regular visitor to the café. If you want to see the lighthouse you have to walk out across a field because the road stops at the car park. If you have travelled this far, it's worth the walk.

We travel back on the south side of the peninsula along the shores of Dunmanus Bay through Kilcrohane, Ahakista and Durrus, where we take a right turn at the top of the village out the Creamery road. This is a lovely road on a bike, with plenty of bends and nice straight parts where you get a chance to look at the scenery. We go straight through at the next crossroads and onto a t-junction where we turn right on the N71. We turn left at the pub in Culloman and then the next right on a small road through Dromore. At the next t-junction we turn left and at the top of the hill we turn sharp right and head for Dunmanway.

Here you can see a wind generating station on a hill on the right hand side of the road so we decided to go up for a look. As we travelled up the hard packed gravel road I was overtaken by Liam on his XJ900 and on the way back down, passed again by both Liam and Patrick, who overtook us both on his Pan. Just remember that I am the fellow on the trail bike!

In Dunmanway we turn left onto the N71, straight through Ballineen, Enniskean, Bandon and 150 miles later we return to Cork.

– B.B.

Cork to the Ring of Beara

Beautiful landscapes and passes

Category: easy, a short bit medium on the Old Mine Road

79/84/85/86

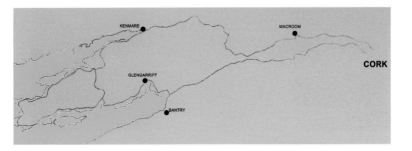

Start at the County Hall in Cork. Drive for approximately 2.5 km on the N22 out of the city, turn at the next crossroads to the right onto the R618 which follows the River Lee to Macroom. Before the town of Macroom turn left on the N22, and then turn right on the R584 through Inchigeelagh alongside Lough Allua to Ballingeary. In the town, turn right to Coolea. Having passed through Coolea, cross the Clydagh River on the Inchee Bridge and proceed along the Roughty River to Kilgarvan.

Proceed on the R569 to Kenmare, in the town turn left and then right on the R571 through Coornagillagh to Derreen and the Healy Pass. In Adrigole right on the R572 through Derreeny, Castletownbere (also called Castletown Bearhaven) to Cahermore. The island on the left hand side is Bere Island. The way from Cahermore to Allihies is along the spectacular Old Mine Road, which is the R575 today, around the Slieve Miskish Mountains.

Before Eyeries turn left on the R571 again to Derreen. Here you jump the Healy Pass again and but turn left this time in Adrigole onto the R572 to Glengarriff. At Glengarriff turn right and take the N71 to Ballylickey, then turn left onto the R585 (which is a good road) to Kealkill. Here turn left onto the R587 to Kilmichael, then right through Teerelton, and then turn left to the River Lee Reservoir (also called Inniscarra Reservoir). Follow the river through Farran Forest Park to Ovens and then join the N22 to Cork.

Cork to Allihies

Scenic landscape, panoramic views
Category: medium, some difficult
79/84/85/86

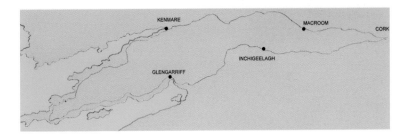

The spin started in the usual place, the filling station by the County Hall on the Carrigrohane Straight at 11:00 a.m. The weather was a little cool but dry, although rain was forecast. Only three of us turned up, as the rest had been away all week on an Irish photographic rally. There was Patrick on his Pan, Richard on his GS1200 and myself on my 1986 R80G/S.

We leave promptly at 11:00 a.m. and head west out on the Carrigrohane Straight. We take the first right turn onto the R618 towards Dripsey. This is a good road with lovely views over Inniscarra Dam and the River Lee. In Dripsey we turn right, in the direction of the Model Village and up past Dripsey Castle. Watch out for the sharp bend on the bridge just after the castle. At the next junction we stay left and then take the first right followed by the next left across from the pub.

We travel west towards Bealnamorive. Even though this road is quite narrow it has some good straight bits so you can get up a bit of speed along here. There is a lovely tower on the left hand side of the road at the end of the straight. We take the second left in Bealnamorive and drive straight through the next few junctions. Next we come to Morris' Bridge, which is a sharp right hand bend over an old narrow bridge. We then come to the junction on the Macroom to Millstreet road. You have to be very careful crossing here, because visibility both ways is bad and the traffic travels quickly on this part of the road. Once across it's a short distance to the next junction.

Here we turn right and travel through Clondrohid to Ballymakeery. This is a good fast road. We turn right onto the N22 through Ballyvourney. Just as we exit Ballyvourney we turn left on the

Coolea road. This is another good road with nice sweeping bends through Coolea and up to Coom where you can find the highest pub in Ireland. As we travel down from here we see the rain clouds out west. When we reach the bottom at Morley's Bridge we turn left on the R569 through Kilgarvan and on to Kenmare. We turn left over Kenmare bridge, then take a right turn on the R571 towards Eyeries. This is a very nice road for a bike with a good surface, a mix of gentle sweeping bends and sharp corners, and stunning views of Kenmare Bay and the surrounding mountains. By now the weather has improved and the sun is shining and we are seeing the countryside at its best.

When we leave Eyeries we take a right turn towards Allihies. A few miles along this road we turn left at the old school house and right turn onto a dirt road. We then have to open a gate to

get onto the Old Mine Road. This road is a hard packed dirt and gravel road, not for the faint-hearted, as it goes very high up the mountain where it leads to the old copper mines. This is well worth the effort for the spectacular views, fresh air, and sense of adventure. From here we travel down a series of hairpin bends to Allihies. The beautiful sandy beach here is also well worth a visit.

From here we travel back on the south side of the Beara Peninsula on the R571 through Castletownbere to Glengarriff for lunch. Again this is a good motorcycling road with plenty of bends and some straight sections where you can get a chance to appreciate the breathtaking scenery.

After a fine lunch we travel at a blistering pace to Ballylickey on the main Bantry road. On roads like this I can really push the cornering capabilities of my R80G/S. At Ballylickey Bridge we turn left onto the R584 through Kealkill, past Gougane Barra to Ballingeary. You can hold the throttle at 60mph through the corners all the way up and through the Pass of Keimaneigh and down the other side. Gougane Barra, as mentioned earlier, is well worth a visit if you have the time.

Just as we approach Ballingeary we take a right turn onto the south lake road to Inchigeelagh. In Inchigeelagh we turn right and then after a couple of miles take a left turn. From here we travel on a series of small roads straight through a number of crossroads, through Kilmichael, Teerelton, Warrenscourt, Kilmurry, and then take a right turn onto the N22 at Crookstown and 176 miles later we are back in Cork.

Another nice day out with friends. It's days like this that you can really appreciate the joys of motorcycling.

– B.B.

Cork to Waterville

Beautiful landscape, scenic views and passes

Category: medium

78/79/80/83/85

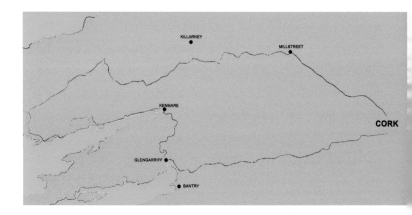

Start at Cork County Hall. Drive in the direction of the city, keep left at the first set of lights, at the second set turn sharp left and turn left again on the R579 to Cloghroe. Turn right to Tower, continue through Matehy and Crean's Crossroads to Rylane Cross, and follow the Kerry Road through Carrigagulla to Millstreet.

In Millstreet turn left at the church, this road leads to the west alongside the Paps to Headfort. There turn left on the R570 to Glenflesk. Drive approximately 0.75 km on the N22 in the direction of Killarney and turn left at the next crossroads. This road brings you alongside Lough Guitane to Muckross. Turn left on the N71 to Moll's Gap and there turn right and right again. Here you drive over the Ballaghbeama Gap to Boheeshil. After

Boheeshil turn left over the Ballaghisheen Pass and then over Lissalinnig Bridge, along Lough Namona and Lough Currane to Waterville. A fantastic route!

It is worthwhile to plan on staying overnight around Waterville, we would recommend the Kenmare Bay Hotel, which is very biker-friendly.

The way back to Cork is on the N70 to Kenmare, then the N71 through Glengarriff to Ballylickey, here turn left onto the R585. From here you can relax and wag the tail (of your bike) to Crookstown. Finally turn right, through Stickstown and Aherla to Cork.

Cork to Kenmare Variation

Panoramic views, scenic landscape and mountains

Category: easy

78/79/80/85/86

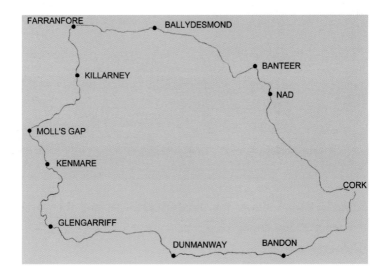

I called for Liam at 10:45am and we made our way out to the filling station next to the County Hall. Here we filled up with fuel and had a quick cup of coffee. It wasn't long before the others arrived. First came Andy on his 1150GS, then Morris on his 1200GS, then Paddy on a 1200GS which he borrowed from Frank. Liam was on his 900 Diversion and I was riding my K1100LT. The plan was to meet Patrick at Farranfore Airport in Kerry and then to go on to Kenmare.

We leave the filling station at about 11:30 and head west out on the Carrigrohane Road. At the end of the straight we turn right

in the direction of Clorough. By the time we got to Clorough the roads have dried up so we pick up the pace. We go straight up through Nad and on to Banteer. Here we turn left on the Mallow – Millstreet road.

By now the tyres are well warmed up and the roads are quiet so we are eating up the miles. We turn right from Rathcool to Cloonbannin and head towards Boherboy and Ballydesmond. The weather is very cold but dry. The K11 is at home on these fast straight roads with long sweeping bends. The road surface is in surprisingly good condition apart from the odd pothole or dipping bump on fast bends. It is a cold crisp February day with good visibility so the countryside looks very well.

At Ballydesmond we head towards Castleisland. When we come to Scartaglin we turn left and then take the next right. These roads are smaller but in okay condition. Very soon we arrive in Farranfore. In the meantime Patrick has landed at the airport and picked up his bike so we meet him here with his Pan European.

The lads insist that we get a coffee because they are frozen. I am quite comfortable as the fairing on the K11 offers very good weather protection and with the heated grips at low position my hands are nice and warm.

From Farranfore we travel south on the N22 to Killarney and on through Moll's Gap to Kenmare. It is very difficult to look at the beautiful scenery when driving this road – there are a lot of corners, traffic, cyclists, pedestrians and sheep! It is better to find a spot to pull over for a look. From Moll's Gap onwards the road is being improved all the time, so it is possible to travel along at a nice pace. In Kenmare we stop for lunch in the Wander Inn. The staff here are nice and the food is very good, especially on a cold February day. An hour later we are back on the bikes ready to go, but Patrick's Pan won't start. After a quick investigation it turns out to be a loose battery connection. The problem is quickly solved and we head south out of Kenmare towards Glengarriff on what's locally known as the tunnel road, because you pass through a tunnel (Turner's Rock Tunnel). The views are spectacular especially shortly after you come out of the tunnel as it is very high up looking out over Bantry Bay. We continue on down to Glengarriff. When we stop I notice that all of us have a big grin on our faces from the exhilarating spin down the mountain. Next we travel on the Bantry road to Ballylickey where we turn left and then take a right turn in Kealkill which takes us up the Coosane

Gap. This road is in very good condition so you can maintain a high speed here. We turn right just before Cappeen and head for Dunmanway. You must be careful on this road because some of the bends are quite severe and if you are still travelling at speed it is very easy to run out of road.

In Dunmanway we turn left on the R586 towards Bandon. We have a heart stopping moment just outside Enniskean when a jeep in front of us decides to do a u-turn without indicating. We stop in Bandon for coffee and to give out about the jeep. Then we head home on the N71 to Cork.

Good weather, good roads and lovely scenery made for a very nice 177 mile trip with friends.

– B.B.

Cork to Dingle

Scenic landscapes, passes and more
Category: medium
70/71/78/79/86

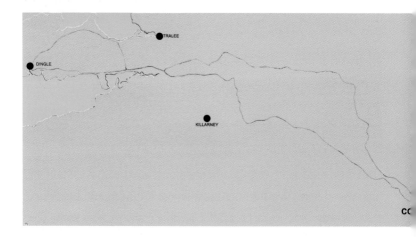

This tour brings you directly to Dingle and the Dingle Bay, one of the most beautiful bays of Ireland with many nice beaches. A variation to the Dingle round trip follows. This route and the next are recommended in combination as a two-day tour.

Start is at the Cork County Hall. Drive in the direction of the city, at the major crossroad turn left and left again on the R579 to Cloghroe. Turn right to Tower, through Matehy and Crean's Crossroads to Rylane Cross, continue along the Kerry Road through Carrigagulla to Millstreet.

Proceed on the R582 to Rathmore. After approximately 4 km take the N72 to Killarney, but before you get there, turn right in

Barraduff to Scartaglin. Follow the sign to Farranfore where you pass Kerry airport. At the next crossroads turn left and at the next cross in Farranfore turn to the right to Dingle.

In Anascaul you should make a stop to see the museum dedicated to the Irish antarctic explorer, Tom Crean. The statue in front of the museum has been erected in his honour.

At the roundabout in Dingle take the third exit to the Connor Pass where there is a panoramic view of Dingle Bay in the south and Tralee Bay in the north. Continue through Ballyduff, Stradbally, Aughacasla and Camp in the direction of Aughils and you will get to the Caherconree Pass with another spectacular view.

The way back to Cork is through Castlemaine, Riverville, Currans, Castleisland and Cordal, where you cross the Blackwater River and turn onto the R578 to Newmarket. From here take the R576 to Kanturk and the R579 to Cork.

Tralee to Dingle

Scenic landscapes, strands and a dolphin

Category: easy

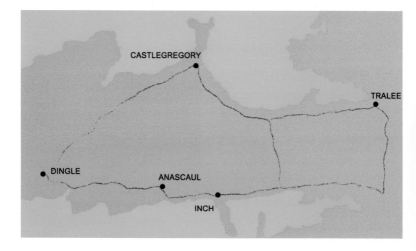

From Tralee drive to Castlemaine alongside the Knockawaddra mountains and you already in the midst of beautiful countryside. Before Castlemaine turn right towards Dingle. Here you'll get to the Inch Beach, Ireland's Daytona Beach and one of the few opportunities in Europe to drive for miles along a beach (legally). To keep it this way there are a few rules: the dunes here are national trust property, so hands (and feet) off. Take your rubbish away with you! (This is the same everywhere, anyway.) No Races! Another important word of advice is that at high tide you will find that it is only suitable for 4x4 vehicles and off-road bikes, everyone else gets stuck. If you get onto the beach at low tide, keep an eye on the waterline and leave well before the water gets

too high – you don't want to be stuck at the very other end at high tide. Also, watch out for soft sand: somersaulting over the front wheel is the last thing you would like to experience on your holiday, so drive slowly.

If you never have experienced this before, you should – a mile long drive on an empty beach until the road behind you is only a mirage in the air ... Cool! As the bay faces west, the sunset on clear days is not only something for the old romantics.

If you can tear yourself away from all this, you'll want to proceed to the west, along the coast to Dingle. In the summer season Dingle is overcrowded with visitors, but nevertheless try to stop in this small town. The aquarium at the harbour is also worth a visit. If you have never stroked a stingray or held a starfish in your hand, you should give it a try!

Dingle Bay came into focus in 1983 because of Fungie. Fungie is a wild dolphin that has chosen to be a regular visitor to the people of Dingle Bay. There are consequently a number of tourist boats offering trips into the bay, on which you hear the stories and speculations on why Fungie has come to stay and perhaps even get to meet the dolphin himself.

The question that bothers me, however, is how long is the life expectancy of a dolphin living in the wild? There are some rumours that the dolphin you meet might be a Fungie of the third generation ... but I'm keeping quiet!

After this you might want to make the roundtrip to the land's end on the R559, starting and ending in Dingle.

There are many beaches on the coast of Ireland. The Carrignaparka at the Dunmore Head is of particular interest because it is below high cliffs, but you can drive the (steep) road down to it. A small waterfall creates a natural shower as you arrive at the beach with sweet water – very handy, especially when you want to wash off the salty water after swimming. If you walk along the cliffs you will find many sheltered corners to spread out a towel ...

The roundtrip should in any case be followed with a drive over the Connor pass. Here you have a gorgeous view over both bays on either side of the peninsula. At Castlegregory you can drive round Brandon Bay to the land's end and continue back to Castlegregory again. You'll get back to Tralee quickly on the N86.

Macroom to the Paps

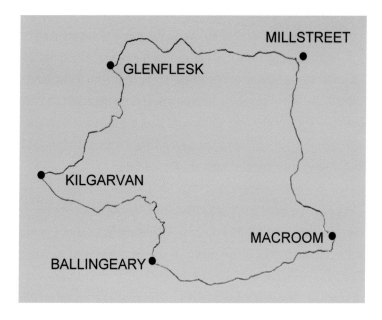

Macroom is suitable for any tour into the historically important West Cork, part of the 'Rebel County'. Many places and monuments here bear witness to the difficult birth of the Irish state. One example is Kilmichael, SSW of Macroom, the place where the 'Kilmichael Ambush' took place.

But West Cork is also well known for the frequency and concentration of monuments of ancient Ireland. Standing stones, stone rings and ring forts can be found everywhere around Macroom. In most cases though, there are neither signs nor information, they are often in the back yard of a farmhouse. If you want to see them just ask permission from the farmer.

This tour starts at the southerly end of the town of Macroom. Turn right onto the R582 in the direction of Millstreet, after about I km turn left to Clondrohid. Even after this short distance you will find standing stones. After Clondrohid keep left, cross the Foherish River, and continue straight ahead at the Townsend's Crossroads. After about 2 km turn right and the road climbs onto the Curraleigh. After the Curraleigh Bridge turn right and then after about I km turn left. Just beyond the Garrane Bridge you'll find a megalithic tomb on the right hand side.

Then turn left onto the R582. Turn left after the Kilmeedy Bridge over the Finnow River and the road climbs the hill again. On this particular road several ring forts and stone circles can be seen. On clear days there is a fabulous view from the slope of the Claragh Mountain. Having crossed the pass turn left at Croohig's Crossroads. This road goes westward alongside the Paps. At Headfort turn left onto the R570, to Glenflesk and Clonkeen.

At Clonkeen turn left onto the R569, in the direction of Kilgarvan. At the Roughty River turn left over the Morley Bridge, and then left again alongside the Roughty River eastwards.

You drive roughly northwards following the southern slopes of the Foilgreana and Cummeenboy. At the next t-junction you turn right to the east again. The road follows the Sullane River

to Coolea Cross. After another 1.5 km turn right, roughly to the south, although this road does later turn eastwards. At the next crossroads turn right and follow the road southwards to Reananerree. Turn right, then take the next left (southwards) to Ballingeary. Here you'll get onto the R584, then turn left to Macroom, and follow the River Lee which widens into a lake before Macroom. If you want to relax with a cup of tea after this drive, you might try Coolcour House, which has a beautiful view.

You'll get there on the R584 alongside the lake. Turn right onto the N22, after about 0.5 km turn right into the driveway up to the house.

Ring of Kerry

Scenic landscape and pass
Category: medium
78

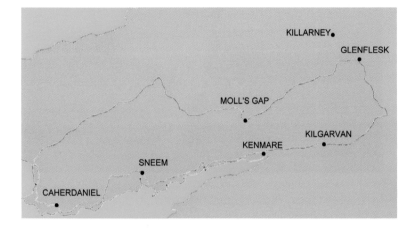

A good tour to do in conjunction with the tour of the Paps is the Ring of Kerry. Ours is a little off the beaten track ...

As the starting point for this tour we have chosen Glenflesk (map 79), about 10 Km south-east of Killarney. After approx. 1.5 km on the N22 turn left to Lough Guitane, you will travel alongside the lake until you reach the Muckross Road (N71) where you turn left to Moll's Gap (on the right hand side you'll see Lough Leane). Turn right onto the Sneem Road, the R568. Take the third road right to the Ballaghbeama Gap (very scenic) – proceed to Glencar, but before coming to Glencar turn left – towards Knocknagapple and over the Ballaghisheen Pass.

If you want to stay overnight here, we recommend looking in Waterville, which is right on the coast. To proceed from Waterville take the Sneem road through Caherdaniel. Staigue Fort, near here, is a place of great historic interest, which you wouldn't want to miss. This circular fort is said to be at least 3,000 years old. It is about twenty-seven metres in diameter and five metres high and surrounded by a ditch. To get there turn right at Castlecove (about halfway between Caherdaniel and Sneem on the N70) onto a small road which leads down to the fort.

Continue through Sneem and follow the coast road to Kenmare. In Kenmare turn left onto the R569, go through Kilgarvan and you get onto the N22. Turn left here and you'll be back in Glenflesk in the blink of an eye.

Cork to Listowel

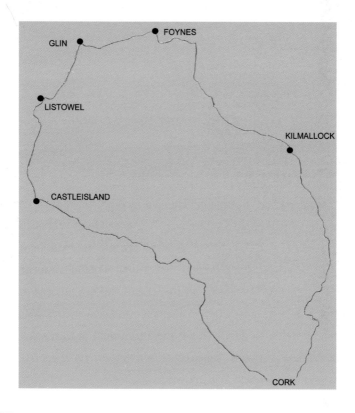

Sunday morning and the sun is shining. I call for Liam at 10:30 a.m., and we make our way out to the County Hall. Five of us turn up: Liam on his Transalp, Andy on his 1150 GS, Morris on his 1200 GS, Frank on his 1200 GS and myself on my 80 GS. The planned spin was Cork to Listowel.

We leave the filling station at 11:10 a.m. and head west on the N22. At the end of the Carrigrohane Straight we turn right and on up through Clorough, Nad and Banteer on the N72 junction where we turn left. At Cloonbannin we turn right and travel up through Boherboy, Kiskeem, Ballydesmond and on down to Castleisland. These are very fast roads and are suitable for all bikes. Castleisland has a one way road system in the centre of the town so we make a left turn up a small road, immediately after the Tralee exit. This is a very straight road with lovely scenery all the way up over the mountain to Six Crosses where we turn right onto the N69 to Listowel. Here we have a nice relaxing lunch and talk about the highlights of the morning run.

After lunch we stay on the N69 and travel very quickly up through Tarbert, Glin, Loghill, Foynes and on to Askeaton. This road is motorcycling heaven with excellent surfaces and breathtaking views of the Shannon Estuary. At Askeaton we turn right onto the R518, through Rathkeale and Ballingarry to the junction of the N20. Having waited a while for traffic to clear we go straight across and travel down to the beautiful village of Bruree where you will see a lovely old mill on your left hand side as you enter the village.

From here we travel down to Kilmallock which is another lovely village with an old abbey and castle. Here we take the R512 through Ardpatrick, Kildorrey and Redmills, where we turn right. We travel through Ballyhooly, Glenville and 186 miles later we are back home.

– B.B.

Cork to Foynes

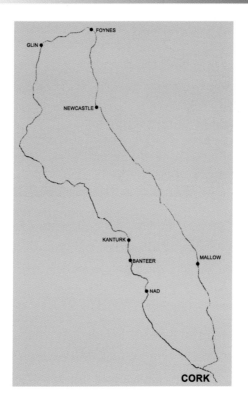

Start at Cork County Hall, travel in the direction of the city, and at the first crossroads turn left and left again to Cloghroe. Take the R579 to Kanturk where Kanturk Castle is worth a stop. Take the R576 through Newmarket to Kilkinlea. After approximately 2 km on the N21 you come to Abbeyfeale and turn left here onto the

R524 to Glin on the shores of the Shannon. Turn right onto the road which follows the shoreline and you will come to Foynes. When you are in Foynes we can recommend the amphibious plane museum.

You can return on the R521 to Newcastle, continue on the R522 through Dromcolliher to Liscarroll. This castle is also well worth a stop. Take the south-westerly road here to Mallow. From here the N20 brings you quickly back to Cork.

Cork to Foynes Variation

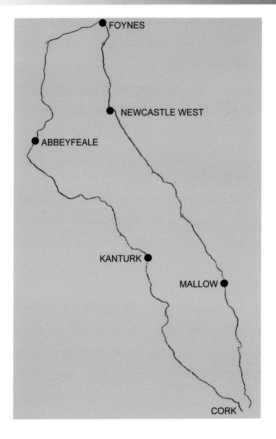

Sunday morning and we wake to clear blue skies and nice temperatures. We start as usual at the filling station at the County Hall. The spin I had planned was Cork to Foynes near Limerick. There were four of us at the filling station by eleven o'clock, Peter on his GS650, Liam on a 1987 Transalp which he had bought the day before, Andy on his 1150 GS and myself on my K1100LT.

We take a right out of the filling station and head towards the city, then the next left, right at the bridge, next left and left again at the grotto. This brings us to Clogheen where we turn right at the church. This is a very fast road all the way to Blarney, where we take a left turn at the t-junction and then second right out to the Waterloo road. At Waterloo bridge we take a right past the round tower and on to Rathduff where we turn left on to the N20 to Mallow.

In Mallow we go straight through the two roundabouts and stop at the filling station where we meet Patrick on his Pan and after a quick coffee and a chat we are underway again. We take the second left turn, under the railway bridge and on to Liscarroll. This is a very fast road, with only two junctions that you have to yield at, and it is practically straight all the way. There are the remains of an old castle on your right hand side as you enter the village of Liscarroll. From here we travel very quickly through Dromcolliher and on the R522 to Newcastle West. Here you have to cross over the R520 on a small bridge then turn right on the N21, then turn left and right where it is signposted to Foynes. This road has an excellent surface and loads of sweeping bends. Very soon we are travelling through Ardagh, Shanagolden and on to Foynes.

At Foynes we drive through the village and turn left into the museum car park. The first transatlantic flights started here in the

1930s and early 1940s. The museum, which is called the Flying Boat Museum, is dedicated to the planes which landed on the Shannon Estuary. It is open every day and is well worth a visit. We went for lunch in a restaurant on the main street, which was okay but not worth recommending.

After lunch we travel west on the coast road through Loghill and onto Glin. This is an excellent biking road with a very good surface, lovely long sweeping bends and fabulous scenery. In Glin we turn left on the R524, through Athea and on over the mountain to Abbeyfeale, where we turn right on the N21. At the bridge in Kilkinlea we turn left on the R576, through Rockchapel, Meelin and on down through Newmarket to Kanturk. At the junction in Kanturk we turn right, over the bridge and take the first left on the R579 to Banteer. From here we travel very quickly through Nad and up over, what's locally known as Nad Bog, down through Cloghroe and back to the t-junction at Carrigrohane.

This is one of my favourite biking roads. We turn left onto the N22 here, and 152 miles later we are back to the County Hall.

– B.B.

'The Big One', a five-day trip

Scenic landscapes, spectacular passes, castles, beaches and cliffs

Category: easy, some medium

63/64/71/72/73/74/78/79/80/81/83/84/85/86/87/88/89

We have started this tour in Castletownroche, where one of the recommended 'where to sleep' places is situated. This castle, whose origins lies in the twelfth century is a great place to spend some stress-free time and recharge the batteries, in particular for a tour like the following one.

Day 1   Castletownroche – Glengarriff

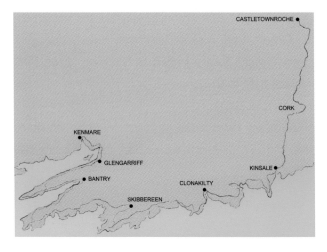

In the centre of Castletownroche turn to the east, in the direction of Fermoy. In Ballyhooly go straight at the crossroads, down the hill where you turn to the right and cross the Blackwater River. At the roundabout go straight ahead and up the hill, take

the next left turn onto the R614, this road brings you through the Nagles Mountains. In Cork the road splits and you keep left onto the R614, the North Ring. Follow the North Ring until the Silver Springs Hotel (on left hand side), here turn left onto the main road which brings you out to the east. After the second roundabout keep to the left of the main road, which brings you to the next roundabout; follow the signs to the airport and you you go under the River Lee through the tunnel which brings you onto the South Ring.

At the next roundabout (after about 5 km) keep to the left and follow the signs to the airport, up the hill on the R600. This road brings you to Kinsale. Having passed Kinsale you stay on the R600 until you get to the R604, where you turn left to the Old Head of Kinsale. Where the road enters the privately owned golf club at the Old Head (no admission to the public) there is a monument on the right hand side commemorating the sinking of the *Lusitania* in 1915 a short way off the coast of the Old Head.

When you get back onto the R604 you'll pass a nice beach on the left hand side, which on hot days makes a welcome break to cool off. In Ballinspittle you'll get back onto the R600, follow it to the left to Castle Gardens. Here turn left to the R601 to Courtmacsherry, Ardgehane and North Ring to Clonakilty. Turn left onto the R598 to Ardfield and Castlefreke, where you can stop to see the castles (Freke Castle and Rathbarry Castle) and the Long Strand Beach with its sand dunes. The R598 brings you further on to Rosscarbery where you turn left onto R597 to Glandore. After Glandore turn left at next crossroads onto the R596 to Union Hall, Rinneen and Baltimore.

Having enjoyed the view over the sea and Sherkin Island just off the coast you might want to go on. Having driven back and out of the village of Baltimore, turn left at the next crossroads and follow the R595 to Skibbereen, turn left here to Church Cross and Ballydehob, from where you take the R592 through Skull,

Toormore and Goleen to the Mizen Head. From here there is a beautiful view of the Fastnet Rock to the south-east of the coast. On the way back, having passed Dough, turn left at the cross and follow the R591 through Dunmanus to Durrus, where you turn left again to Ahakista, Kilcrohane and Ballyroon towards the Sheep's Head. Here you can enjoy a fantastic view over Dunmanus Bay in the south, Bantry Bay in the north and the Atlantic Ocean in the west. To go any further you have to return to Kilcrohane, where you turn left to Gouladoo, League Point and Bantry. A short visit to Whiddy Island might be worthwhile. Otherwise, you probably want to proceed to Glengarriff on the N71 to end the day in one of the nice B&Bs.

Day II Glengarriff – Kenmare

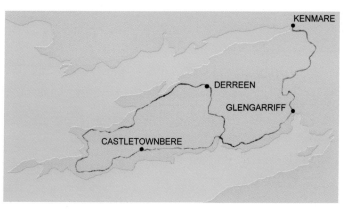

Turn left on the R572 all along the south coastal line to Derreenacarrin, Trafrask, Adrigole, Derreeny and Castletownbere. Proceed on the R575 which takes you around the peninsula to the north side. If you have time, you might do the excursion from

Cahermore to Kilmichael, the head of the peninsula, otherwise you drive through Cahermore, Ballydonegan, Allihies and over Travara Bridge, after which you turn left on the R571 to Eyeries, Ardgroom to Lauragh. Turn right here onto the R574 which brings you to the Healy Pass where you'll find another beautiful view. Back in Adrigole, turn left to Glengarriff, here turn left on the N71 to Kenmare.

Day III   Kenmare – Ring of Kerry – Kenmare

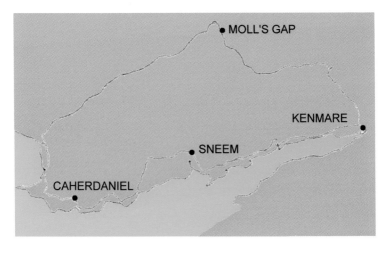

As you probably want to stay the next night in the same hotel, you can enjoy this day without luggage, which you can leave here and this will make your bike easier to handle – a definite advantage on this trip.

All along this route there all sorts of ancient celtic traces, like standing stones, stone circles, cillins and many others. You will

find them marked in the 1:50.000 maps of the Ordnance Survey and it might be worthwhile to put in a stop or two.

Turn left onto the N70 Ring of Kerry route, through Reen, Blackwater Bridge, Parknasilla, Sneem and Castlecove to Caherdaniel, all along the beautiful and scenic coastline. As you are here, you might want to take the opportunity to visit Lamb's Head, and on the way there you will pass another castle ruin. On the north side of the Derrynane Bay you will find the entrance to a very fine beach.

If you can tear yourself away from here, or if the weather isn't good enough to lie on the beach, you might want to proceed to Waterville through the Coomakesta Pass – a very scenic part of the route. In Waterville you can either continue on the route or make an excursion to Ballinskelligs. At the Inny Strand there is usually good surf, which explains the surf school here – if you like to give it a try, they have wetsuits and boards for rent.

Otherwise, turn right in Waterville to Caherbarnagh, this small road takes you up to the Ballaghisheen Pass which has a beautiful view. At the Bealalaw Bridge, turn to the right to Boheeshil, from here you continue to the Ballaghbeama Gap, Dereendarragh and the Moll's Gap. Turn right again here, this road will bring you back to Kenmare again.

Day IV   Kenmare – Listowel

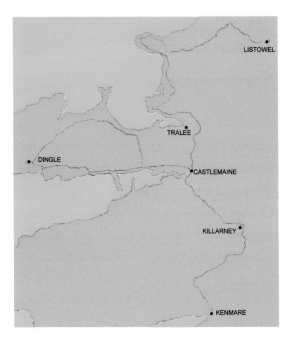

This day starts as it ended yesterday – take the road back up to the Moll's Gap, but turn right this time, this route takes you to the lady's view, a beautiful spot to take pictures. Further on you will drive alongside the beautiful Lough Leane. Muckross House on the left is worth a visit.

Killarney is a tourist town and therefore can be quite crowded during the season. Turn left in the centre onto the R562 and shortly afterwards right on the R563. This road takes you to Milltown where you turn right and then left in Castlemaine on the R561 to Dingle. On the way there the Inch Strand on the left hand side is a beach you cannot pass without having made at least a spin on it. In Anascaul you should look into Tom Crean's North Pole Museum. Dingle itself is always worth a stop, not only for the aquarium in the harbour but also, if you're lucky, as you might get a glance at Fungie, as I mentioned earlier. If you like, you can take an excursion from here along the coast further west where there are some very nice beaches.

Otherwise, the tour proceeds to the Connor Pass: it is signposted at the only roundabout in Dingle. You'll be rewarded with a spectacular view over Dingle bay in the south and Tralee Bay

in the north. Continue through Ballyduff, Kilcummin, Stradbally, Aughacasla and Camp and you will come back to Aughils, turn left here back to Castlemaine where you turn to the left, and shortly after keep to the left again. At the next crossroads go straight ahead and you will come to the outskirts of Tralee. Keep straight ahead again and turn left at the next crossroads onto the R551. Keep to the right on the R551, continue through Ardfert and you will come to Banna, where Banna Strand might make a pleasant stop. At Ballyheige keep straight ahead and then go straight ahead again at the next junction, this road will take you anti-clockwise around Kerry Head. Having fulfilled the roundtrip, turn left after Ballyheige and right at the next crossroads where you follow the R551 until you cross the Cashen River. Then turn to the right at the next cross, over Oaghley to Listowel.

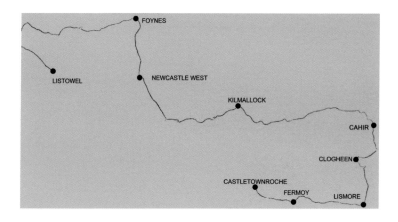

The last day of this big roundtrip begins with the short run to the mouth of the Shannon on the R553 to Ballybunion. From Ballybunion you follow the waterline over Kilconly, Beal, Astee, Ballylongford, Saleen and Tarbert to Glin (here you can see Glin Castle). Further alongside the Shannon you get to Foynes. Here you turn onto the R521 through Shanagolden, Kilcolman and Ardagh to Newcastle. In Newcastle follow the sign to Limerick but just at the end of the village of Newcastle turn right on the R522 to Feohanagh and Dromcolliher. Here turn left onto the R515 to Milford, Charleville and Kilmallock. In Kilmallock turn to the right on the R512 to Blackpool, then turn left here on the R517 to Kilfinnane. In Kilfinnane make sure that you go straight ahead to Ballylanders and then straight on into the Glen of Aherlow which you follow all the way to Cahir. In Cahir take the R670 southwards until you come to the next crossroad, where you turn to the right on the R665 to Clogheen. Here turn to the left on the R668 which brings you up to the Vee with a spectacular view

over the County Tipperary. Further on, down the hill, turn to the right (unless you want to visit the medieval Lismore and Lismore Castle, then go straight ahead at the crossroad) on the very nice R666 to Fermoy. Then there is only the last bit on the N72 over Ballyhooly back to Castletownroche.

Take your time to chill out, you deserve it!

Where to sleep

In general, most of the B&Bs you'll find on the way will be more than comfortable for one night's rest or more. Therefore, we don't really feel that we need to make special recommendations. There are plenty of books and lists available on this subject. We would like to make a few exceptions for some very special places however.

The Blackwater Castle in Castletownroche

An ideal base camp for day-trips in the south of Ireland.

Amenities: self-catering apartments; rooms in the castle with B&B; camping (tents only); drying room for wet gear, washing machine and dryer.

Special services: Tour recommendations and tour guiding. In the castle you will find tour printouts, it is also possible to book tours guided by locals. We recommend early booking, as these tours are very popular. Minor and some major repairs can be solved in the garage here. Breakdown recovery. Open all year; owners are motorcyclists.

Tel: ++353 22 26 333
Fax: ++353 22 26 567
web: www.blackwatercastle.com   email: bwc@iol.ie

... And by the way, one of the authors of the book lives here ...

The Kenmare Bay Hotel
As the owner is an enthusiastic biker, fellow bikers are more than welcome.
Tel: ++353 64 41300
Fax: ++353 64 41541
Kenmare, Co. Kerry   www.leehotels.ie

The Rainbow Hostel
Situated west of the town of Dingle it is a good place to stay if you want to enjoy the area for longer than just a day, camping possible.
Tel: ++353 66 9151044
Fax: ++353 66 9152284
Milltown, Dingle, Co. Kerry www.net-rainbow.com

What you should see

As all the following places have been mentioned more than enough in various travel books, we will just mention the most pertinent details here to give you a flavour of what's around. If you want to learn more about anywhere there is more than one way to find out: of course you can go to the local tourist office but perhaps the most educational (!) is to go into the pub and ask! You might learn about things you won't find in any travel book ...

Ballybunion

At the mouth of the Shannon you'll find the small village of Ballybunion. What makes Ballybunion particularly special are the caves in the cliffs – most of them accessible only by boat at low tide. The path alongside these scenic cliffs – between Doon Cove and Doon Point, which passes Lick Castle – is also a popular destination.

Bantry

The climate in Bantry Bay is influenced by the gulf stream and gives a mediterranean feel to the local vegetation in this beautiful seaside town. Bantry House and Park are certainly worth seeing, as is the valuable art collection within. The stables are also worth a look.

The ruins of an old fortress stand on Whiddy Island, a short ferry ride from Bantry, The purpose of the fortress was to defend the land from attack coming from the direction of the sea.

Blarney Castle

Blarney is to be found north-west of Cork, not far from the city and is well signposted. The remains of Blarney Castle are not very different to hundreds of other square towers around Ireland. What is different is the legend of the castle: he who dares to hang backwards at a height of 100 metres – of course with assistance from the guide – and to kiss the Blarney Stone (like millions of people before him) will be blessed with the gift of eloquence. The guide will be glad to explain the origins of the legend. There are also many good souvenir and knitwear shops in the grounds.

Bunratty Castle and Folk Park

A huge open-air museum. Buildings from different centuries of Ireland have been collected and rebuilt in the park to make a complete village. The highlight is the castle itself, with authentic furniture from the fourteenth century. You can dine in medieval style there, but you must pre-book. Bunratty Castle is situated between Limerick and Shannon airport on the N18.

Cahir

Cahir Castle is one of the mightiest in Ireland. The oldest parts of the castle were built in the thirteenth century and the extensions in the fifteenth century, although it is documented that there was a fortification there in the third century. The castle was regarded as invincible but in 1599, after just ten days of fighting, its defenders had to surrender to the Earl of Essex.

About 6 km north of Cahir is Knockgraffon Motte, an Anglo-Norman fortification from the twelfth century, the ruins of a church from the thirteenth century and the ruins of another castle from the sixteenth century. South of Cahir is Ardfinnan Bridge over the River Suir where there is the ruins of another castle.

Cashel

The prominent Rock of Cashel, north of the village of Cashel, is visible from afar. In earlier times it was the site of kings and in the fourth century was donated to the church and turned into a monastery. St Patrick christened King Aengus here in 450 and Brian Boru declared Cashel his main site in 977. It was rebuilt in 1686 after fires in 1495 and 1647, but was subsequently abandoned in 1749. Now it is an impressive ruin. Cashel, near the N8, is situated between Mitchelstown and Port Laoise.

Cliffs of Moher

The steep cliffs of Moher are always an impressive sight, rising about 120 metres high out of the sea – at O'Brien's Tower they rise to 200 metres. The cliffs are definitely worth a stop, especially in stormy weather when the waves crash against the stones, but also in calm weather when you can watch the numerous seabirds or catch a view of the Aran Islands from the tower.

Cork

Cork is the second biggest city in the republic. Although it is the starting point for many of our tours, the city itself is worth more than one visit. Many regard this town as the 'real' capital of Ireland, make up your mind yourself! The old city of Cork is situated on an island between two channels of the River Lee. You can get a good view of it from St Patrick's Hill.

Cork has been a university city since 1845. Although St Finbarr founded a priory there in the seventh century, the city of Cork really started with the coming of the vikings in the year 917.

Just off Grand Parade and Patrick Street you'll find the old market hall: the English Market, which is built in Victorian style. Every kind of food is available, from wonderfully fresh and exotic fish to succulent chocolates. Also worthwhile is a cup of coffee (or tea) in the café on the first floor. Sitting above the market you can enjoy the view of the hurly-burly underneath, and enjoy the music from the café's marvellous pianist, who tries to compete with the noise below.

St Patrick's Street and Oliver Plunkett Street are the most popular places to go for any kind of shopping and since the smoking act has taken effect there are many street cafés which entice you in for a cup of coffee while watching the streetlife.

As Cork has much more to offer, it might be advisable to visit the tourist office in the Grand Parade where you can find more information on the city and what's on.

Fota Island Wildlife Park

The park is not a zoo, as most of the animals are allowed to run free. The most dangerous thing you will experience is when the begging hordes of apes jump on you; beasts of prey and other endangered animals are of course safely behind the fence. Fota Island is east of Cork, a short distance away on the N25 in the direction of Cobh; you'll find it well signposted.

Cobh

Cobh is well worth a visit, as is the heritage centre in the town. Most emigrants departed for America from the harbour of Cobh in the nineteenth century. Cobh is situated on the Great Island on the opposite side of the bay to Cork. To get there it is a short drive eastwards on the N25.

Glengarriff

In this area the gulf stream takes its full effect which means you will find more tropical-like vegetation here than anywhere else in the north-west regions of Europe. Glengarriff is a small village which has dedicated itself to tourism, so you will find a large

range of B&Bs. Of the many islands in the bay, Garinish Island is the most worthwhile visiting – there are beautiful gardens and also the house in which it's said George Bernard Shaw wrote most of 'Saint Joan' in 1923.

Halfway Vintage Club

Halfway is situated beside the N71 from Cork to Bandon. Turn right at the roundabout after the bridge near Ballinhassig and about 200 metres on the right hand side is the Ramble Inn. In the yard behind is the club. The pub is worth a visit, not least because of the many photos on the wall. This vintage club is representative of the many clubs and groups of vintage car owners and bike enthusiasts all over Ireland. During summer season it is packed every weekend with vintage runs, rallies, events and much more.

Kenmare

Kenmare is situated at the mouth of the Roughty River, although the actual bay is called Kenmare River. Close to the bridge in the town is Cromwell's Fort – although Cromwell himself never was here. Near the bridge, over Finnihy River is a 'circle of druids', a stone circle of fifteen stones with a diameter of fifteen metres.

Killarney

Killarney is situated in the south-west of Ireland. Owing to the attractiveness of the surrounding landscape, the lakes and many other leisure attractions, Killarney is a very popular place to go, Be prepared for crowds during the holiday season.

Not far from the town is Ross Castle, built in the sixteenth century. In 1652, General Ludlow used trickery to capture the castle: it had been prophesied that the castle could only be captured from the lakeside, so he mounted a cannon on a big boat and bombarded the castle from the lake. The defenders then believed the prophecy was being fulfilled and surrendered.

Following the N71 around the lower lake to Muckross Lake you might want to visit Muckross House. The writer of the *Stories of Baron Münchhausen,* Rudolph Erich Raspe (1737–94), used to live here. Also the Kerry Folk Life Museum on the same grounds is worth a look.

Kinsale

Kinsale is a picturesque town, with many of the buildings dating to the eighteenth century. In 1601, the Spanish fleet moored in the harbour of Kinsale. An army of a couple of thousand Spanish soldiers, together with the Irish, fought against the English, but had to surrender to them. As a result English sovereignty over Ireland was sealed. Near Kinsale at Summer Cove is Charles Fort (1677) and the lighthouse. From here James Fort, on the opposite shore, can be seen.

Lismore

There are several places of interest in Lismore, such as the beautiful stone bridge over the River Blackwater, which dates from 1775 and Lismore Castle, which was built in the twelfth century, probably on the previous site of a monastery from the seventh century.

8 km west of Lismore on the R666 is Ballyduff Castle, which dates to 1628. 7 km east of Lismore is Cappoquin, a popular place for fishing. Don't miss the Hindu Bridge here, erected by English soldiers who served in India.

Macroom

The market square of Macroom is surrounded by some nice Georgian houses. Nearby are the ruins of Macroom Castle which was burned down during the troubles in 1922. East of Macroom, at the R618, is Carrighadrohid Castle, which is situated on an island in the River Lee reservoir. Most of the roads leading out from Macroom are scenic routes.

Youghal

Youghal has a very beautiful beach. One of Youghal's mayors was Sir Walter Raleigh (1552–1608) and it is said that it was here the potato was planted for the first time in Ireland, and it then spread out over the rest of the island. South-east of Youghal is Ardmore, a small village with nice beaches. The round tower of Ardmore, built in the twelfth century, is one of the best preserved in Ireland. Close to the tower is the ruin of St Declan's Church, built in the thirteenth century.

Motocross at Castlelyons

Coming from Fermoy towards Cork you turn left in Rathcormack to Castlelyons. Not far from Castlelyons (southwards from the village about 4 km and well signed) you'll find a gorgeous motocross track. For twenty euros (currently) you can rev up for the whole day. Unfortunately, rental bikes are not available.

Car boot sale in Castletownroche

In Castletownroche every second Sunday Ireland's biggest car boot sale is held. On these days it is quite likely that you'll end up in a traffic jam while trying to drive through the town. Nevertheless, it is well worth having a look around and meeting people from all around Ireland.

The Blackwater Valley

The Blackwater Valley offers a wide range of outdoor pursuits such as horse-riding, walking, fishing, football, soccer, road bowling, quad biking, karting and many more. The Blackwater Heritage Trail leads you through the towns and villages of Mallow, Killavullen, Castletownroche, Ballyhooly, Rathcormack, Castlelyons, Bally-volane, Conna, Curraglass, Tallow, Lismore, Cappoquin and back over Ballyduff, Clondulane, Kilworth, Glanworth, Labbacalee, Fermoy, Doneraile, Buttevant, New Twopothouse and Mallow again. On this trail you can see castles, abbeys, old mansion houses, horse fairs, steeplechases, priories, churches, towers, ancient ringforts and wedge tombs – depending on the season in some cases, of course.

For friends of gardening there is also a Blackwater Valley Garden Trail which takes you to the most stunning gardens.

If you want more information on the heritage and garden trail, you should visit the following website:

www.blackwaterholidays.com

A note about ancient Ireland

As you travel through Ireland you cannot fail to notice the stone circles, standing stones and so on, so here are some brief historical notes about them that you may find of interest. It is thought that all life on this island dates from about 13,000 years ago, the approximate date of the final retreat of the great ice age. A minor ice age returned destroying nearly all life. This icy mantle finally disappeared about 10,000 years ago, or 8,000 BC. The age into which the land emerged is called the Mesolithic, or the middle stone age.

It is thought that the history of man in West Cork begins around 6,000 BC. In two areas not far removed, on the coast of Co. Kerry and along the Blackwater River in East Cork the evidence of early hunting/gathering people have been found.

Most visible traces originated in the Megalithic Age, which literally means 'Large Stone' Age. Stone circles, standing stones and many other monuments can be seen in the landscape of today which date from this time. In modern archaeology the Megalithic Age is held to begin during the Neolithic period and last until the Bronze Age, between approximately 4,000 and 1,000 BC. It is assumed that most monuments which have been found in West Cork are from the period 2,500 to 1,500 BC.

Stone circles are the most common and widely recognised phenomena from the Megalithic period. However, experts are still unable to agree on the meaning and function of these stone circles: some refer to their astronomical orientation as their prime purpose, while others see them as burial places. Standing stones or gallanes are the most numerous of all the prehistoric structures to be found in the landscape of Ireland. Numerous single stones and alignments (i.e. more than one and up to six standing stones) are to be found in West Cork, and it is assumed that there were even more, but many have been removed, knocked down, buried or used to make walls.

It is not known if these stones had an astronomical purpose or why most are set on a south-west–north-east alignment.

Cromlechs/wedge tombs and also dolmens are found in different sizes in Ireland, from small table-sized structures to massive rocks of fourteen feet in length and breadth or considerable constructions such as the 'Callaheenacladdig' at Ahaglaslin, near Rosscarbery into which a person can walk without stooping.

In the maps of the Ordnance Survey 1:50,000 Discovery Series most of the Megalithic objects are listed and a short excursion from the route is always worthwhile.

'Butter on the road'

Although known as the 'Butter Road', these roads were built long before the butter market was a commercial proposition in these parts. The Butter exchange wasn't established until twenty years after the road was finished and only became a viable business after England removed the legislative restrictions on the importation of butter. The road was actually built when Killarney was becoming an interesting place to visit and it made sense to build a road to it from the second largest city in the country, i.e. Cork. Of course there were roads already, but they were all in such a terrible condition that the construction of a new road seemed the most practical option.

It was the Irish entrepreneur John Murphy who built the Kerry Road. Using his own money and some borrowings, he had the

road built between 1747 and 1748. It's said that his plan was to make his fortune with the road toll he could collect.

The act of 26 February 1747 stated that John Murphy was entitled to have the right to collect the road toll from 1 May 1748 for sixty-one years. This date is thought to be the birth of the Kerry Road.

But fate was against John Murphy: high interest rates on his loans and losses as a result of farmers running off with toll money caused him to sink into debt. The situation worsened as new bridges were built which would divert many of the people who had travelled on his road – as well as their toll money. After a petition made to the parliament, Murphy was allowed to collect toll money inside the towns which his road crossed. But the carrying of butter to Cork was not yet the trade it became when the Butter Exchange was established in Cork in 1770. This would eventually have been a good source of income for John Murphy, but it came too late to save him. It is unknown what happened to Murphy in his later years.

The construction of a straight road was revolutionary in these times but there were good reasons for building it this way: it was the shortest distance between two points and also facilitated easier travel as drivers could sleep and the horses would not go astray as they tend to always walk straight ahead. Also, horses find it easier to travel on hilly surfaces being easier on the muscles than flat surfaces.

On 1 May 1998, the 250th anniversary of the Kerry Road/Butter Road was celebrated. A memorial tablet in remembrance of John Murphy was installed at the Kerryman's Table.

Always expect the unexpected

This is an old Irish truth. The following incident is a good example. I was out finding new routes near Macroom on a rainy late summer day. I saw three motorcycles beyond a bridge on a right hand bend, two of them were evidently quite old. I stopped to have a closer look at them and learned from their owners that they were taking part in a vintage rally. During the conversation it transpired that one of them was the organiser of the rally and

he invited me to join them. What followed was a fantastic tour among about thirty beautifully maintained vintage bikes (and their drivers, of course), an invitation to lunch, and a lasting friendship with some of these enthusiasts. I regularly meet some of them to go on a spin on the most beautiful tours in the south of Ireland.

This and other events confirm that life on the 'green island' is rather unusual.

I hope that every visitor experiences the magic of Ireland and takes some of the fairytale home from their mystery tour.

Travelling to Ireland

The most common way to get to Ireland, coming from the continent, is to either take the direct ferry from France to Cork or Rosslare, or to take one of the ferries crossing the channel or the channel tunnel and cross England (preferably on the M4) to Wales and take one of the ferries over to Ireland from there.

Travelling by ferry

As prices, departure times and ferry routes can vary from season to season, it is advisable to check information on the internet. Taking a little time here can save a lot of money. Coming from the continent we recommend the 'landbridge-tariffs': package deals from the continent which entail crossing England to get to Ireland. These tickets should be booked well in advance.

Company	Website	Destinations
P&O Ferries	www.poferries.com	Continent – UK
P&O Ferries	www.poirishsea.com	UK – Ireland
Stenaline	www.stenaline.com	UK – Ireland
Irish Ferries	www.irishferries.com	UK – Ireland
Brittany Ferries	www.brittanyferries.com	France – UK/Ireland
Condor Ferries	www.condorferries.com	France – Channel Islands/UK
Hover Speed	www.hoverspeed.com	France – UK
Seafrance	www.seafrance.com	France – UK
Seacat	www.seacat.co.uk	UK/Isle of Man – Ireland
Seacat	www.steam-packet.com	UK/Isle of Man – Ireland

Eurotunnel (train)	www.eurotunnel.com	France – UK
Norfolk Line	www.norfolkline.com	France – UK
DFDS	www.dfdsseaways.com	Scandinavia – UK/Holland
Fjord Line	www.fjordline.com	Norway – UK/ Denmark
Swansea Cork Ferries	www.swanseacorkferries.com	UK – Ireland
Transmanche Ferries	www.transmancheferries.com	France – UK
Wightlink Ferries	www.wightlinkferries.com	UK – Isle of Wight
Norse Merchant	www.norsemerchant.com	UK – Ireland
Northlink Ferries	www.northlinkferries.co.uk	Scotland only
Red Funnel Ferries	www.redfunnel.com	UK – Isle of Wight

Apart from booking well in advance to save money, you should have no problems in getting a place on a ferry at short notice, unlike travelling with a car.

The transportation of the bike and yourself all the way by train onto the ferry to Ireland is recommended only to those who do not need to worry about cost.

Arriving by air

Flying to Ireland and then renting a bike is difficult, if not impossible. The cost of insuring bikes in Ireland is currently too high to allow companies to provide bikes at affordable prices. Therefore, there are very few motorcycle-rental companies. Nevertheless, if you choose to fly here you will find quite a few airlines who offer flights to Ireland at amazingly low fares if you can plan and book early in advance. Otherwise you may find that prices during the tourist season can be extremely high.

Very last words

It is quite likely that routes and roads may change, roads may be closed and new ones built. That is very much in the nature of these things. If there have been any vital changes in one of the routes this was not foreseeable at the time of publication. I am grateful for any hints, criticism and suggestions. So it only remains for Barth and I to wish you a lot of fun on your way around Ireland. And do always expect the unexpected – but in the most positive sense!

If you wish to contact me you may use my email address. Any comments you may have are very welcome:

patrick@nordstroem.com

If you wish to book a tour guided by Barth you may write to the same address.

Céad míle fáilte go Éire